Slithering Snakes

Sarah Creese

make believe ideas

Slithering snakes have scaly skin.
They can climb up trees and even swim!
With a flickering tongue they taste the air.
Now let's explore them—if you dare!

Copyright © 2010 make believe ideas ltd.
27 Castle Street, Berkhamsted, Hertfordshire, HP4 2DW.

Reading together

This book is an ideal first reader for your child, combining simple words and sentences with stunning color photography of real-life snakes. Here are some of the many ways you can help your child take those first steps in reading.
Encourage your child to:

- Look at and explore the detail in the pictures.

- Sound out the letters in each word.

- Read and repeat each short sentence.

Look at the pictures

Make the most of each page by talking about the pictures and finding key words. Here are some questions you can use to discuss each page as you go along:

- Why do you like this snake?

- What would it feel like to touch?

- What color is it?

- Does it look friendly or scary?

Look at rhymes

Some of the sentences in this book are simple rhymes. Encourage your child to recognize rhyming words. Try asking the following questions:

- What does this word say?

- Can you find a word that rhymes with it?

- Look at the ending of two words that rhyme. Are they spelled the same? For example, "hot" and "spot," and "trees" and "seas."

Test understanding

It is one thing to understand the meaning of individual words, but you need to make sure that your child understands the facts in the text.

- Play "find the obvious mistake." Read the text as your child looks at the words with you, but make an obvious mistake to see if he or she catches it. Ask your child to correct you and provide the right word.

- After reading the facts, close the book and think up questions to ask your child.

- Ask your child whether a fact is true or false.

- Provide your child with three answers to a question and ask him or her to pick the correct one.

Quiz pages

At the end of the book there is a simple quiz. Ask the questions and see if your child can remember the right answers from the text. If not, encourage him or her to look up the answers.

Snakes

Snakes can live in many different places around the world, from deserts to the sea.

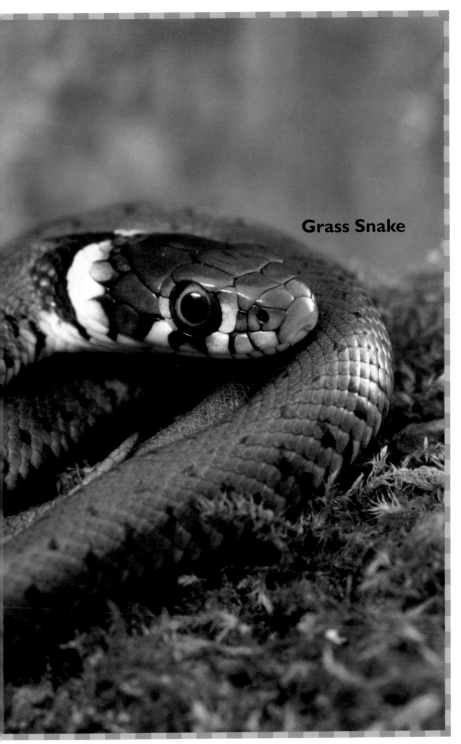

Grass Snake

I'm a slithering snake
with no arms or legs.
I can be long or short
and I can lay eggs.

Hatching Green Tree Python

Green Tree Python

To warm up,
I lie somewhere hot.
To cool down again,
I find a shady spot.

Garter Snake

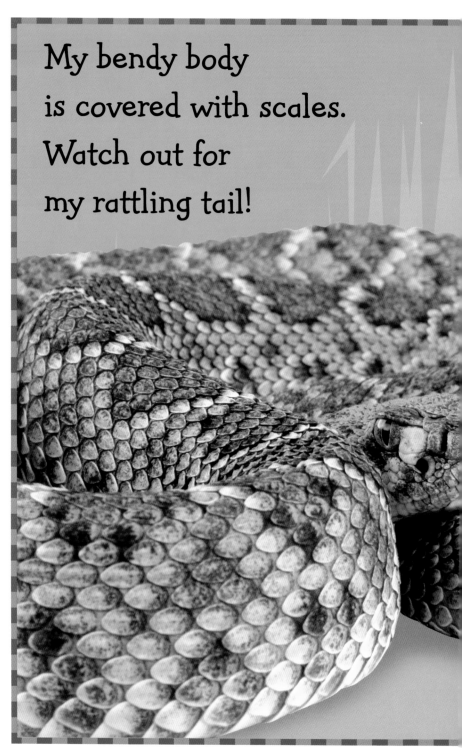

My bendy body
is covered with scales.
Watch out for
my rattling tail!

tongue

eye

mouth

**Western Diamondback
Rattlesnake**

rattle

13

Northern Watersnake

I live on land,
in deserts and trees.
I can swim underwater
and live in the seas!

15

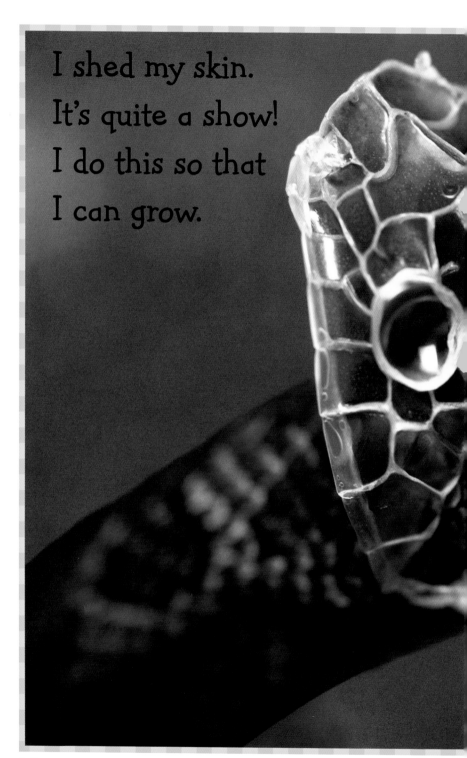

I shed my skin.
It's quite a show!
I do this so that
I can grow.

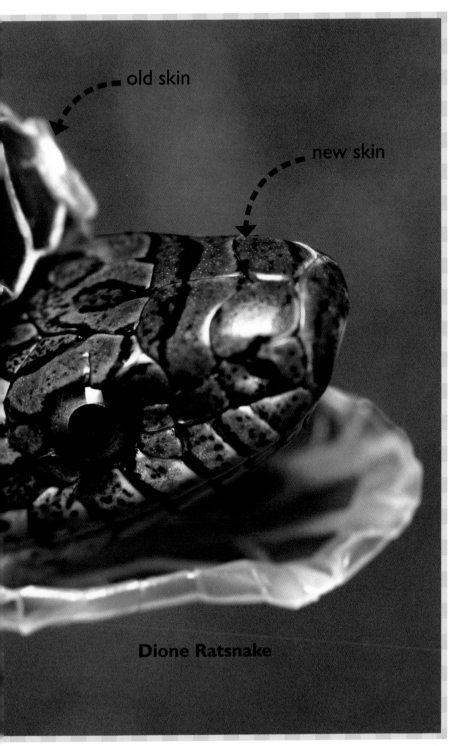

old skin

new skin

Dione Ratsnake

Boa Constrictor

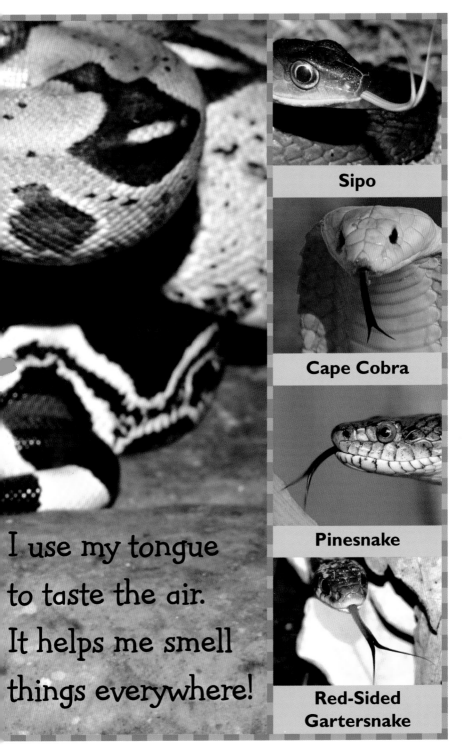

I use my tongue
to taste the air.
It helps me smell
things everywhere!

Sipo

Cape Cobra

Pinesnake

**Red-Sided
Gartersnake**

Egg-Eating Snake

I'm an egg-eating snake.
Can you tell?
I swallow eggs whole,
then spit out the shell!

Egg is swallowed whole

Egg bulges in snake's bo

Egg breaks

Snake spits out the shell

Milksnake

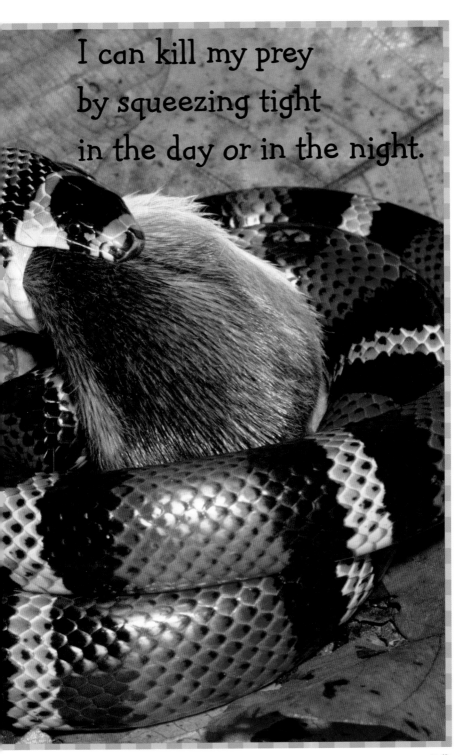

I can kill my prey
by squeezing tight
in the day or in the night.

I can stretch my mouth
to eat a whole deer!
When I'm feeling hungry,
it's best to keep clear.

Grass Snake

Southern African
Rock Python

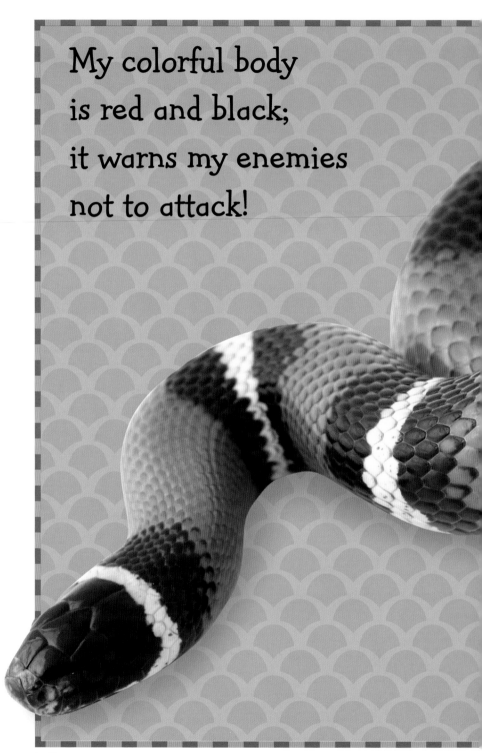

My colorful body
is red and black;
it warns my enemies
not to attack!

Milksnake

What do

1. What do snakes use to smell?

Snakes use their tongues to smell.

2. Why do snakes shed their skin?

Snakes shed their skin in order to grow.

3. How do snakes warm up?

Snakes warm up by lying somewhere hot.

you know?

4. Which snake eats eggs?

The egg-eating snake eats eggs.

5. How do snakes cool down?

Snakes cool down by lying somewhere shady.

6. What type of skin do snakes have?

Snakes have scaly skin.

Useful words

stretch
When you stretch, you make your body wider or longer.

desert
A desert is a dry, sandy land that is hot during the day and cold at night.

slither
Snakes slither by twisting their body and moving smoothly.

shed
When snakes shed their skin, they lose their old skin to reveal new skin.

shady
A shady place is somewhere cool and dark.